Properties of Matter

by Gregory K. George

PEARSON
Scott
Foresman

DK

What is matter?

Properties of Matter

Matter is anything that has mass and takes up space. All living and nonliving things are made of matter. Scientists use the properties of matter to identify it. Your senses can help you find many of these properties. You can see the color, size, and shape of some matter. You can touch matter to tell if it is smooth or rough. You can taste and smell some matter too.

Testing Matter

You can also test matter to find out about its properties. How does it react if you heat or cool it? Is it affected by a magnet? Does electricity pass through it? If you hit it with a hammer, does it break or just bend? If you put it in water, does it sink or float? What happens if you mix it with other matter?

Look at the ice and water. What are some properties that you can see?

States of Matter

Matter is made of tiny particles. These tiny particles can move. They are also arranged in different ways. The way these particles move and the way they are arranged tell the form, or state, of the matter. The most common states of matter are solid, liquid, and gas.

Most substances are found in just one state in nature. Water is the most common substance that can be found naturally in all three states of matter.

Solids

solid

An ice cube is solid water that forms at temperatures of 0°C or below. A solid is any kind of matter that has a definite shape and takes up a definite amount of space. The particles of a solid are packed closely together.

Liquids

liquid

Water is a liquid. A liquid is any kind of matter that has no definite shape but takes up a definite amount of space. The particles of a liquid are not packed as closely together as particles are in a solid. The particles can slide past each other.

Gases

gas

Water vapor is an invisible gas. Water vapor and other gases make up the air around us. A gas is any kind of matter that has no definite shape and does not take up a definite space. The particles of a gas are not close together. They move in all directions.

5

How is matter measured?

Mass

You weigh more on Earth than you would on the Moon. Why is that? Weight depends on the force of gravity. The Moon has less gravity than Earth does. So your weight on the Moon would be less than it is on Earth.

Mass does not change. Mass is the amount of matter an object has. Since mass stays the same wherever an object is, measuring mass is useful for scientists. Mass changes only if matter is added or taken away.

23 grams

The mass of the toy is equal to the total mass of its parts. The pan balance is level.

Using a Pan Balance

A pan balance helps you find the mass of an object. You can use a pan balance to compare a mass that you know with one that you do not know. The masses are equal when the two sides are level.

The mass of the toy in the picture is 23 grams. What if you took the toy apart and measured each part? The mass of all the parts would add up to 23 grams. The total mass of the parts is equal to the mass of the toy that is put together.

The pan balance shows this. The toy is on one side of the pan balance. It is in many pieces on the other side. Both sides have a mass of 23 grams. The masses are equal. This would be true even if all of the pieces were put together in a different way.

Metric Units of Mass

Scientists do not use ounces and pounds to measure matter. They use metric units. The base unit of mass in the metric system is the gram (g). Other metric units that are often used are the milligram (mg) and the kilogram (kg).

The metric system is based on tens. A prefix before a base unit changes what it is worth. For example, 1 gram is the same as 1,000 milligrams. A mass of 1,000 grams is the same as a mass of 1 kilogram. A grape has a mass of about 1 gram. A cantaloupe has a mass of about 1 kilogram.

The mass of the milk in this carton is about 1,000 g, or 1 kg.

The mass of a nickel is about 5 g.

The mass of a large paper clip is about 1 g.

8

Volume

Volume is the amount of space that matter takes up. When you take a deep breath, your lungs expand. As they fill with air, their volume increases.

You can use a metric ruler to measure the length, width, and height of a solid, such as a box. To find the volume, multiply these numbers together. Suppose the length of a box is 6 centimeters (cm), the width is 2 cm, and the height is 5 cm. Then the volume of the box is 6 cm $\times$ 2 cm $\times$ 5 cm, or 60 cubic centimeters.

Like mass, volume is also measured in metric units. Scientists use metric units such as the cubic centimeter (cm^3) and the cubic meter (m^3) when they measure solids. Look at the chart to see some other metric units.

Comparing Metric Units of Length

Metric Unit	Equivalent
1 millimeter	0.001 meter
1 centimeter	10 millimeters
1 decimeter	10 centimeters
1 meter	100 centimeters or 1,000 millimeters
1 decameter	10 meters
1 hectometer	100 meters
1 kilometer	1,000 meters

9

Volume of Liquids

Unlike solids, liquids do not have exact shapes. So when scientists measure the volume of a liquid, they use a measuring container, such as a graduated cylinder. Some metric units used for volume are the milliliter (mL) and the liter (L). A graduated cylinder is marked with milliliters. One liter is the same volume as 1,000 milliliters.

The water level rose 5 mL when the ball was dropped in. The volume of the ball is 5 mL.

Volume of Other Objects

A graduated cylinder can measure the volume of a liquid or a solid. A solid must sink in water in order for a graduated cylinder to measure it. To measure the volume of a ball, fill a graduated cylinder with water. Notice the height of the water. Then put the ball in the water. Notice the new height of the water. It is higher because the ball has pushed away some of the water. The number of milliliters the water has risen is equal to the volume of the ball. A volume of 1 mL is the same volume as 1 cm^3.

Examples of Metric Lengths

What Was Measured	Measurement
Thickness of a CD	1 mm
Length of a paper clip	32 mm
Thickness of a CD case	1 cm or 10 mm
Height of a doorknob from the floor	1 meter
Length of a school bus	12 meters
Length of 440 blue whales placed end to end	11 km or 11,000 m
Distance from the North Pole to the equator	10,000 km

Density

You may need to know how much mass is in a certain volume of matter. Does steel have more mass than wood? To find out, you need to know the sizes of the pieces of steel and wood. You need an equal volume of the objects you are measuring. **Density** is the amount of mass in a certain volume of matter. If the pieces of wood and steel are the same size, then the steel has more mass and more density than the wood.

Finding Density

You divide the mass of an object by its volume to find its density. Like mass and volume, density is measured in metric units. The units to measure density are grams per cubic centimeter. Density is written as a fraction: $\dfrac{\text{mass in grams}}{\text{volume in cubic centimeters}}$ or $\dfrac{g}{cm^3}$.

Cooking oil

Water

Corn syrup

Comparing Densities

The density of an object tells if the object will sink or float in a liquid. Some liquids float on other liquids. As you can see in the picture, water floats on top of corn syrup. The density of water is less than the density of corn syrup. Cooking oil floats on top of water. So the density of cooking oil is less than the density of water.

The grape is floating on top of the corn syrup and at the bottom of the water. This is because the density of the grape is less than the density of the corn syrup, but more than the density of the water. The cork has the least density of anything in the container.

The density of an ice cube is a little less than the density of water. This means that an ice cube will float in water. But the difference in density between water and an ice cube is very small. So most of a floating ice cube is below the surface.

How do substances mix?

Mixtures

A **mixture** is a blend of two or more substances. These substances can easily be separated. They are not chemically combined.

Think of a bag of frozen vegetables from the store. The vegetables have been combined into a mixture. But they can be separated. When the vegetables are separated, they have the same properties that they had before they were mixed.

Look at the mixture of marbles, beads, sand, safety pins, and salt. How can these parts be separated? Safety pins are attracted to a magnet. So you can use a magnet to pull out the safety pins. Then you can put the mixture in water to help separate what is left. The beads float to the top. You can use a spoon to take those out. Then you can pour the rest of the mixture through a filter. The filter will separate the sand and the marbles from the liquid. You can evaporate the liquid by heating it. Then the salt will be left.

The properties of each of the substances do not change when the mixture is separated. Each substance is the same as it was before it was added to the mixture.

Solutions

Salt and water stirred together make a mixture. But you cannot see the salt in the water. The salt has dissolved. It has broken into very small parts. The salt and water have made a special mixture called a solution. A **solution** is made when one or more substances are dissolved in another substance.

The most common kind of solution is a solid dissolved in a liquid. The substance that is dissolved is the **solute.** In a solution of salt and water, salt is the solute. The substance that takes in the other substance is the **solvent.** In the salt and water solution, the water is the solvent. Ocean water is a solution.

The salt is dissolved in this solution.

Salt dissolves in water.

salt

Common Solutions

A solution does not have to be a liquid. The air we breathe is a solution made of gases. Steel used for buildings and cars is a solution of carbon and iron.

Solubility

Solubility measures how much of a substance will dissolve in another substance. Sand does not dissolve in water. This means the solubility of sand in water is zero.

By raising the temperature of a solvent, you can dissolve a solute faster. It is easier to dissolve sugar in warm water than in cold water.

Crushing a solute also makes it dissolve faster. A sugar cube will dissolve slowly in a cup of water. The sugar cube will dissolve faster if it is crushed first.

Sand does not dissolve in water.

sand

17

How does matter change?

Physical Changes

Origami is the art of folding paper to make shapes. When you do origami, you do not change the particles of the paper. You are only changing the size and shape of the paper.

Any change in the size, shape, or state of matter is a **physical change.** In a physical change, the particles that make up matter do not change. It is the arrangement of those particles that changes.

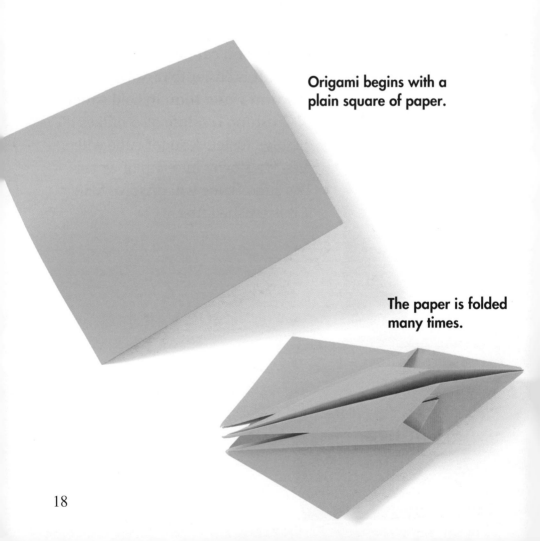

Origami begins with a plain square of paper.

The paper is folded many times.

Mixing salt and water is a physical change. The particles of the salt and the water do not change when they mix. Salt and water make a mixture. The parts of a mixture do not change, and they can be separated. So making a mixture is a physical change.

Another example of a physical change is breaking a pencil. The pieces of a broken pencil have the same kinds of particles as a pencil that is in not broken.

Tearing a sheet of paper is also a physical change. No matter how many pieces the sheet of paper is in, it still has the same particles that it had before it was torn.

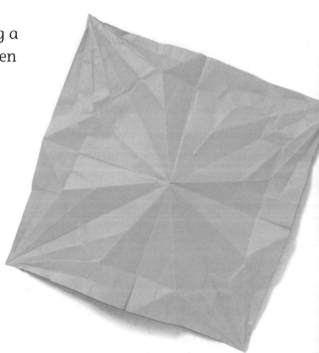

If you unfold the shape, you will have the same piece of paper you started with.

The shape is finished.

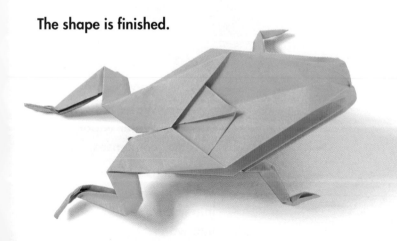

19

Phase Changes

Water can be a liquid, a solid, or a gas. If you melt solid water, or ice, it becomes liquid water. If you heat water to a temperature of 100°C, it becomes a gas, or water vapor. Liquid, solid, and gas are called phases.

What causes matter to be in one phase and not another? Energy causes particles to move faster and farther apart. Adding or taking away energy causes a substance to change phases. You add energy to water when you heat it. You take energy away from water when you freeze it. Phase changes are physical changes.

Effects of Temperature on Matter

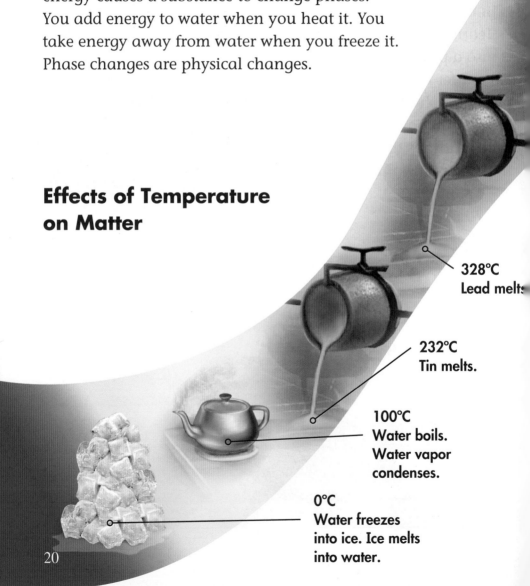

328°C
Lead melts

232°C
Tin melts.

100°C
Water boils.
Water vapor
condenses.

0°C
Water freezes
into ice. Ice melts
into water.

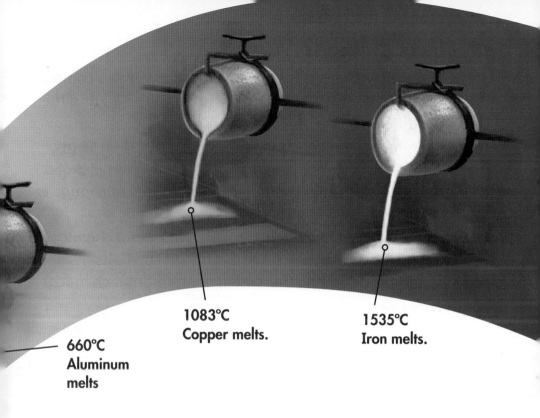

660°C
Aluminum
melts

1083°C
Copper melts.

1535°C
Iron melts.

Every substance changes phases at a different temperature. The melting point or boiling point is a physical property. Each helps identify a substance. Ice melts at 0°C. Lead melts at 328°C. A substance melts and freezes at the same temperature.

A substance evaporates and condenses at the same temperature too. Evaporation is the change from a liquid to a gas. Condensation is the change from a gas to a liquid.

When water evaporates or condenses, it is changing phase. The particles of ice are close together. They do not move much. Adding heat adds energy. The particles move more. Ice becomes a liquid. Boiling water has even more energy. Particles move even more. The liquid water changes to water vapor.

Chemical Changes

An iron nail will rust if it is in a damp place. If you compared the iron nail to the rust, you would find that the nail and the rust have different properties. Rust is a new, different substance. It results from a chemical change. In a **chemical change,** particles of one substance are changed to make particles of a new substance with different properties. A chemical change is taking place when wood burns or silver tarnishes.

The color of a substance may be different after a chemical change. The substance may have a different smell. Its temperature may change. Heat often comes from a chemical change.

The Periodic Table

Rust forms as oxygen combines with the iron in this gear.

Burning wood reacts with oxygen to form ashes, carbon dioxide gas, and water vapor.

Elements

All particles in a pure substance are alike. The simplest pure substances are elements. Information about the elements is in a chart called the Periodic Table. The row and column the element is in tells scientists about its properties. Each element has a letter or letters as its symbol.

Elements are matter. In fact, everything is made of matter. All matter can be measured. You can find out the mass, volume, or density of any kind of matter. All matter can go through chemical and physical changes.

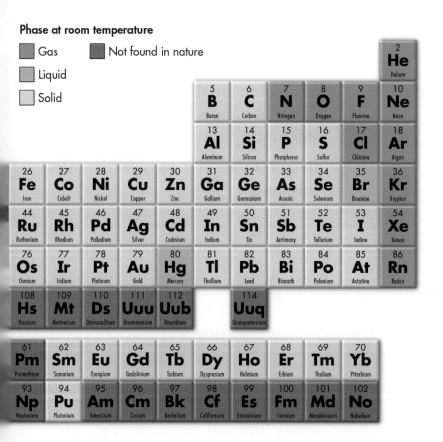

Phase at room temperature

Gas Not found in nature

Liquid

Solid

Glossary

chemical change   a change that occurs when the particles of one substance change to make particles of a new substance with different properties

density   the amount of mass in a certain volume of matter

mixture   a blend of two or more substances whose properties do not change when they are combined

physical change   any change in the size, shape, or state of matter

solubility   a measure of how much of a substance will dissolve in another substance

solute   the substance that is dissolved in a solution

solution   a combination that results when one or more substances are dissolved in another substance

solvent   the substance that dissolves another substance